# Angels

New and future titles in the series include:

Alien Abductions

Angels

The Bermuda Triangle

The Curse of King Tut

ESP

Haunted Houses

UFOs

Unicorns

Witches

The Mystery Library

# Angels

Patricia D. Netzley

Lucent Books, Inc.
P.O. Box 289011, San Diego, California

*For Matthew, Sarah, and Jacob, who believe*

Library of Congress Cataloging-in-Publication Data

Netzley, Patricia D.
    Angels / by Patricia D. Netzley
        p. cm. — (The mystery library)
    Includes bibliographical references and index.
    ISBN 1-56006-768-3 (alk. paper)
    1. Angels—Juvenile literature. 2. Demonology—Juvenile
literature. [1. Angels.] I. Title II. Mystery library (Lucent
Books)
    BL477 .N48 2001
    291.2'15—dc21

00-009442

# Contents

# Foreword

In Shakespeare's immortal play, *Hamlet*, the young Danish aristocrat Horatio has clearly been astonished and disconcerted by his encounter with a ghost-like apparition on the castle battlements. "There are more things in heaven and earth," his friend Hamlet assures him, "than are dreamt of in your philosophy."

Many people today would readily agree with Hamlet that the world and the vast universe surrounding it are teeming with wonders and oddities that remain largely outside the realm of present human knowledge or understanding. How did the universe begin? What caused the dinosaurs to become extinct? Was the lost continent of Atlantis a real place or merely legendary? Does a monstrous creature lurk beneath the surface of Scotland's Loch Ness? These are only a few of the intriguing questions that remain unanswered, despite the many great strides made by science in recent centuries.

Lucent Books' Mystery Library series is dedicated to exploring these and other perplexing, sometimes bizarre, and often disturbing or frightening wonders. Each volume in the series presents the best-known tales, incidents, and evidence surrounding the topic in question. Also included are the opinions and theories of scientists and other experts who have attempted to unravel and solve the ongoing mystery. And supplementing this information is a fulsome list of sources for further reading, providing the reader with the means to pursue the topic further.

The Mystery Library will satisfy every young reader's fascination for the unexplained. As one of history's greatest scientists, physicist Albert Einstein, put it:

> The most beautiful thing we can experience is the mysterious. It is the source of all true art and science. He to whom this emotion is a stranger, who can no longer wonder and stand rapt in awe, is as good as dead: his eyes are closed.

# Introduction

# A Fascination with Angels

According to several surveys, approximately 70 percent of Americans believe that angels are real beings, 50 percent believe that they have their own personal guardian angel, and 30 percent think that they have actually encountered an angel on earth. Angels have also been featured prominently in four major religions: Zoroastrianism, Judaism, Christianity, and Islam. Yet there has never been definitive proof that angels exist—or has there?

Stories of encounters with angels abound in modern times. Books like the Rev. Billy Graham's *Angels: Ringing Assurance That We Are Not Alone*, Eileen Freeman's *Touched by Angels*, and Sophy Burnham's *A Book of Angels* and *Angel Letters* provide many such stories, and in every instance people who have had angel encounters are adamant that the experience was real and changed their lives. For example, Eileen Freeman tells of one man who was climbing down a cliff when he realized he was going to fall. Knowing he would be killed if he lost his grip, he prayed for help, and suddenly he saw angels around him holding him against the cliff. He then felt them lift him up, and within a few minutes he was safe on top of the cliff, with no memory of having climbed its face.

There are also many stories of people who did not see an angel but believe that an angel helped them nonetheless.

For example, in the early 1950s, all fifteen members of the choir in the West Side Baptist Church in Beatrice, Nebraska, were late for their regularly scheduled choir practice. Although they were trying to get to the church separately, some little incident happened to each one that delayed that person's arrival. Consequently, no one was in the church when, three minutes after choir practice would have begun, the building's heating system malfunctioned and caused an explosion that destroyed the entire structure. Had any choir members arrived on time, they would have been killed. Today, people in the town and those who have studied angel encounters generally believe that angels were responsible for the delays that saved all fifteen lives.

*In most modern stories, angels are helpful beings.*

In most modern stories of angel encounters, angels are helpful beings. However, when angels were first written about in ancient times, they were either fierce beings who destroyed God's enemies or benign beings who delivered messages for God without becoming involved in individual people's lives. Where, then, did the idea for helpful angels come from? And if angels do exist, what do they look like? Where do they live? What do they do? Are all angels good, or are some of them bad?

For answers to these questions, modern people have turned to ancient religious scriptures, ancient and medieval writings on angels, and stories of angel encounters throughout history. They have also relied on artists' interpretations of religious scriptures, which have helped define the appearance and nature of angels. Collectively, human beings have developed firm ideas about angels—although whether or not these ideas are correct is a matter of speculation dependent on faith.

# Where Did Angels Come From?

Diverse cultures share a belief that angels are spiritual beings who act as intermediaries between humans and a deity. Because of this common belief, some people think that the idea of the angel arose in one place and then spread elsewhere. Others believe that the idea sprung up in many places at once—perhaps on the basis of visitations by angels who wanted to encourage people's faith.

## Earliest References

The oldest reference to a being that could be considered an angel is an image on a stele—a large, upright engraved stone slab or pillar—that dates from approximately 3000 B.C. Located in the ruins of the ancient city of Ur near Babylon (now part of Iraq), the stele shows a winged figure descending from the heavens to pour water into a king's cup. The ancient Sumerians who carved the religious figure believed that the water was the essence of life, and they viewed the winged creature not as a god, but as a servant of the gods. Although this creature was not called an angel, it had the same appearance and relationship to the deity as angels in other cultures.

*This 2300 B.C. stone carving depicts beings that could be considered the first images of angels.*

The same was true for the ancient Greek god Hermes, a winged messenger. Although Hermes was a deity himself, his purpose was to serve other gods just as an angel would. Some scholars have suggested, therefore, that it was the concept of Hermes that inspired the Greeks to translate the Hebrew word for one of God's heavenly servants—malakh, or "one sent"—as *angelos*, which means "messenger." It is from *angelos* that the English word *angel* is derived.

Ancient Hindus also had gods that sometimes functioned as messengers for higher gods. Called devas, these gods are considered by some scholars to be roughly equivalent to angels. In fact, among modern practitioners of a nineteenth-century religious philosophy called Theosophy, which combines elements of Eastern and Western religions, the words *deva* and *angel* are interchangeable. However, according to traditional Hindu thinking, devas have much more independence and responsibility than angels, with control over various aspects of the natural world.

## Zoroastrianism

The first reference to a true angel occurred in Persia (now Iran) during the emergence of a religion called Zoroastrianism. This religion was founded by the prophet Zoroaster, also known as Zarathustra. Scholars disagree on when this took place; some say it was in 1000 B.C. or earlier, while others argue that it was around 600 B.C. Zoroastrianism remained the main religion of Persia until the seventh century A.D., when the region was taken over by Islam, and today is practiced only in Iran and a small part of India.

Prior to the development of this religion, people believed that there were many gods, all of whom deserved worship. But Zoroaster argued that there was a supreme god—Ahura Mazda, also known as Ormazd—who ruled everything, although he was opposed by another god—the evil Angra Mainyu, also known as Ahriman. Zoroaster claimed that an angel named Vohu Manah ("Good Mind") had visited him to tell him about these two gods. He urged people to stop worshiping many gods and to pray instead only to Ahura Mazda.

But early Zoroastrians had difficulty abandoning the gods they had formerly worshiped. Therefore, they transformed many of these beings into angels who helped Ahura Mazda run the world. For example, the god Vata, or Vayu, became the angel in charge of the winds. The Zoroastrians also came up with new angels who performed various duties, such as Mithra, the angel of light and truth, who was almost as powerful as Ahura Mazda. The Zoroastrians prayed to all of these angels, thereby retaining their old system of worshiping many gods even as they embraced Zoroaster's new religion.

Zoroastrians also placed some of their former gods in the category of demons who helped the evil Angra Mainyu rather than Ahura Mazda. The ancient Persians believed that there would one day be a final battle between the forces of good and the forces of evil, after which people would be judged worthy or unworthy by being placed into a river of fire. Worthy people would then be melted down to their purest essence, while unworthy people would be totally consumed.

*Zoroaster argued that Ahura Mazda, depicted here in a relief sculpture, was the supreme god who ruled everything.*

## Zoroastrian Influences on the Hebrews

The idea of battling good and evil angels spread to the Hebrew people after 539 B.C., when the Persians conquered the Babylonians, who had previously conquered the Hebrew land of Judah in 597 B.C. Zoroastrianism was then practiced in Babylonia as well (modern Iraq). But modern scholars are not entirely agreed on whether the Hebrews already believed in angels prior to their exposure to Zoroastrianism.

Many of the books that make references to the Hebrew Bible—a book known to Christians as the Old Testament—were written before any Persian influence; however, it is uncertain whether later copyists of the Bible inserted these references. In particular, some scholars argue that whenever the Hebrew Bible mentions that an angel spoke to a human being, that angel was really God himself. These scholars believe that the people who copied the Old Testament over the years were uncomfortable with the idea of God talking directly to people, and so they inserted an angelic intermediary.

As evidence to support their theory, these scholars point to several biblical passages where it seems that the words "angel of the Lord" and "God" are used to refer to the same being. For example, in the Book of Exodus, the Hebrew leader Moses encountered a bush that burned with a miraculous fire. In referring to this bush, Exodus 3:2 says that "the angel of the Lord appeared unto him [Moses] in a flame of fire." Two verses later, Exodus 3:4 adds: "God called unto him [Moses] out of the midst of the bush." Consequently, some people believe that both God and an angel were in the bush, while others believe that only God was there and the reference to the angel is a copyist's alteration.

Other scholars have alternative explanations for these passages. Some stories may be combinations of different versions, one in which God appeared and another in which an angel appeared. Also, since angels were regarded as divine beings and spoke the words of God, they may sometimes have been referred to as "God."

## The Cherubim

The first appearance of an angel in the Hebrew Bible is also a matter of controversy. It occurs in the first book of the Bible, Genesis, which is traditionally said to have been written by the Hebrew leader Moses in approximately 1250 B.C. but which most scholars believe was written centuries later. According to Genesis, after God commanded the first humans, Adam and Eve, to leave the Garden of Eden, angels called cherubim stood guard at the garden's entrance to keep the couple from returning. Genesis 4:23–24 says:

> Therefore the Lord God sent him [Adam] forth from the garden of Eden, to till the ground from whence he was taken. So he drove out the man; and he placed at the east of the garden of Eden Cherubims, and a flaming sword which turned every way, to keep the way of the tree of life.

The word *cherubim* comes from the Akkadian language, which was spoken by many different groups of people living in Mesopotamia (modern Iraq). It means "ones who pray," or "ones who intercede," and it was originally used to refer to half-human, half-animal creatures who stood guard at the entrances of temples. That both the word and the concept of a temple guard appear in a biblical passage from before the period of Persian influence seems to suggest that the Hebrews drew on other religious traditions even before the establishment of Zoroastrianism. But, again, it is difficult to know when this word was first used in the Old Testament, the original text of which has been lost.

*Scholars debate the words of the Bible which refer to the being that Moses encountered as both an angel and God.*

## Guards, Warriors, Messengers

What is apparent, however, is that the earliest biblical references to angels primarily place them in the role of a fierce guard or a warrior. As an example of the latter, in the Second Book of Kings, God sent an angel into the camp of some Assyrian soldiers who were planning to attack the Hebrews. The angel's mission was to kill everyone in the camp during the night. 2Kings 19:35 says:

And it came to pass that night, that the angel of the LORD went out, and smote in the camp of the Assyrians a hundred fourscore and five thousand: and when they arose early in the morning, behold, they *were* all dead corpses.

Again, some scholars argue that it was not the angel of the Lord, but God himself who killed the Assyrians. But regarding later books of the Old Testament—ones that were clearly written after the Hebrews had come into contact with Zoroastrianism—no such arguments can be made, because there is a definite distinction between God and his angels. At the same time, the primary role of an angel has changed from God's warrior to God's messenger.

There are many examples of angels bringing God's words to the Hebrew people. At first these messages were personal and affected the lives of just a few people. For example, in Genesis, one of the early books of the Old Testament, three angels (or God and two angels, according to some scholars) visited the Hebrew patriarch Abraham and his wife, Sarah, to tell them that Sarah would soon give birth to Isaac—a miraculous piece of news given that both people were in their nineties at the time. But in later books of the Old Testament, angelic messages concerned the fate of nations and were generally given to prophets to pass on. For example, in the Book of Daniel, an angel appeared to the Hebrew prophet Daniel to help him interpret a vision sent by God, which used symbolism to foretell the conquest of the Persians by the Greeks.

## Varied Influences

According to James R. Lewis and Evelyn Dorothy Oliver, two modern experts on religious beliefs, in *Angels A to Z*, the Book of Daniel is the part of the Old Testament most influenced by Zoroastrianism. They say:

The final books of the Hebrew Bible, particularly Daniel, reflect the distinct influence of Persian angelology [beliefs about angels]. As a result of several centuries of Persian control of the Middle East, Jews were brought into contact with Zoroastrian religious ideas . . . [particularly] Zoroaster's doctrine of the ongoing struggle between good and evil—a dualistic world view that included war between good and evil angels.[1]

*This rendering depicts Zoroaster, the founder of the religion Zoroastrianism, whose beliefs influenced other religions.*

Consequently, there are references to this battle in the later books of the Old Testament, as well as in other Jewish writings from the late ancient period that did not become part of the Hebrew canon, or list of accepted scriptures.

The most significant of these other writings, in terms of angels, are the *Book of Enoch* and the *Book of the Secrets of Enoch*, sometimes referred to as *1 Enoch* and *2 Enoch* or as the *Ethiopic Enoch* and the *Slavonic Enoch*. The latter two names refer to the languages into which the oldest known complete copies of the books were translated.

Scholars believe that the *Books of Enoch* first appeared sometime between 200 B.C. and 200 A.D. as part of a group of writings referred to by Protestants as the *Pseudepigrapha*. The word *Pseudepigrapha* means "books falsely attributed"; the writings in this collection were originally—and incorrectly—believed to have been written by biblical figures. Enoch, for example, was mentioned in the Hebrew Bible as being a descendant of Adam and the father of Methuselah, a man said to have lived 969 years, longer than anyone else on earth.

Enoch was popularly believed to have risen directly into Heaven without dying. Accordingly, the books about him go into great detail about the activities of angels. They tell of approximately two hundred angels who went to earth, originally to help create the Garden of Eden. While there, these angels developed a physical attraction to the first women to inhabit the earth and fathered a race of giants called the Nephilim. The angels committed many other sins as well, thus angering God so much that he punished them and banished them permanently from Heaven. The books also say that God's favorite angel—Satan— placed his throne higher than all the rest and was punished for his pride by being cast out of Heaven. He then became the leader of the banished, or fallen, angels on earth.

Because many people originally believed that the *Books of Enoch* were written by a biblical figure, they believed in them, along with another book that expanded on the Enoch stories. Called the *Book of Jubilees*, this book says that God created his great flood (the one that prompted Noah to build his Ark) specifically to wipe out the Nephilim. But early leaders of the Christian Church felt that stories about sinful angels who fathered a race of giants were in poor taste, and some of them argued that it was impossible for an angel, who was entirely spirit, to father children anyway. Consequently, the Church decided to eliminate the *Books of Enoch* and the *Book of Jubilees* from the canon. These books were not read openly and for many years they were lost. Today, Catholics refer to them as Apocrypha, a word that means "hidden books."

## The Nature of Christian Angels

But although the *Books of Enoch* and the *Book of Jubilees* were hidden, their ideas remained a part of the Hebrew culture—a culture which early Christians drew upon in establishing their own religion. Consequently, Christians believe that a group of sinful angels was once expelled from Heaven. Perhaps more importantly, Christianity embraced Enoch's view of Satan and his angels as separate beings with free will rather than as servants of God who act as extensions of his will. The idea that angels can act counter to God's will is one of the most important legacies of Zoroastrianism, in which angels are based on pagan gods, who originally had minds of their own. In early Hebrew writings, no angel stands in opposition to God. In later writings, angels are sometimes disobedient, and Satan is as evil and as powerful as Angra Mainyu.

But while Christian angels sprung from Zoroastrian beliefs, it was not long before they were infused with new and unique qualities. Beginning around 500 A.D., with a Syrian scholar who called himself Dionysius the Aeropagite (the name of a New Testament figure) and is often referred to as Pseudo-Dionysius, or "false Dionysius," to distinguish

*In 1635, Thomas Heywood wrote* The Hierarchie of the Blessed Angels, *one of many books written about angels.*

him from the original Dionysius, Christians theorized that angels had specific duties based on their position in a hierarchy of angels. Dionysius identified nine choirs, or divisions, of angels, each succesive with a higher level of power and responsibility than the preceding one. In describing the attributes and duties of these categories of angels, he gave them distinct personalities and defined their nature more thoroughly than previous writers. Other Christians soon added to Dionysius's work, and by the Middle Ages there was a rich body of Christian literature devoted to angels and their nature.

The main scripture of Christianity, known as the New Testament, also includes many references to angels—far more than the Old Testament. Moreover, angels have more prominent roles in the New Testament than they do in the Old. For example, an angel named Gabriel brings the news to Mary that she is to be the mother of Jesus Christ, the central figure in the Christian religion. Many Christians believe that Mary became an angel herself after her death and/or became the leader of all the angels in heaven.

Another important angel to Christians is Michael, who is believed to be God's warrior. Many Christians believe that Michael was the one who personally expelled Satan from Heaven, and many think that Michael will be the one to defeat Satan in a future war between good and evil angels. Like Zoroastrians, many Christians are certain that this war is destined to take place, along with a Judgment Day during which individual people will be deemed either worthy or unworthy to be with God.

Angels are an important part of Christian theology, and at various times in history, Christians' veneration of good angels has been excessive. In response, Christian churches have sometimes forbidden their members from paying so much attention to angels, fearing that people would begin worshiping them much like pagan gods. Christian churches have also devoted much energy to dissuading people from worshiping Satan, whom many Christians believe is a real being. To many Christians, Satan is not only the leader of the fallen angels but also a tempter of humans, who either personally or through his servants convinces people to turn away from God. Meanwhile, good angels work to convince people to keep following God's teachings.

## Mormons

Most Christians believe that although both good and bad angels visit earth to either help or harm human beings, they are not and never have been human beings themselves. They are nonhuman, wholly spiritual creatures—not ghosts or any other embodiment of the human soul—who live with God in Heaven but can take on the appearance of a human if necessary. One denomination of Christians, however, believes differently. Mormons, who belong to the Church of Jesus Christ of Latter-Day Saints (LDS), think that angels are resurrected people who often have real human bodies.

Non-Mormon scholars believe that Mormons might have gotten this idea from cultures that feature flesh-and-blood gods. Some of the Hindu devas, for example, are said to have evolved from human beings whose souls were reincarnated through several lifetimes. Mormons themselves, however, deny that their beliefs were derived from any Eastern religion. Instead, they say that they were given their beliefs by an angel named Moroni, who visited the founder of their religion, Joseph Smith, one night in 1823.

According to Smith, Moroni provided the location of a book of scripture, the *Book of Mormon*, that was buried in New York State in the fifth century A.D. by descendants of Nephi, a figure who lived in biblical times and sailed to America. The *Book of Mormon* is the basis of the Mormon faith, and it includes many stories about angels. For example, it mentions three Nephites (the term for descendants of Nephi) whom God allowed to live on earth after death as helpful angels in human bodies. The angel Moroni is said to be a resurrected human, the son of the last leader of the Nephites.

*Mormons believe that the angel Moroni was a resurrected human.*

## Islam

Because of the belief that the *Book of Mormon* was provided by an angel, a belief in angels is perhaps more critical to Mormons than to any other denomination of Christians. Angels are also fundamental to the religion of Islam for the same reason: it was an angel who inspired the creation of the faith.

Islam is practiced primarily by people living in countries in the Middle East and North Africa. Until the seventh century A.D., these people believed in many gods. Then, in the year 610, an Arabian prophet named Muhammad went on a spiritual retreat in a mountain cave near Mecca and was visited by an angel whom he later identified as Gabriel. In this and subsequent visitations, Gabriel brought Muhammad the message that there was only one God and gave him a series of revelations regarding God's teachings. Muhammad was told to recite these teachings to others, and eventually they were written down in a book known as the Koran (or Qur'an), which means "reading" or "recitation."

There are many connections between the Koran and the Old and New Testaments of the Bible. For example, like the Bible, the Koran says that the first humans were Adam and Eve, cast out of the Garden of Eden for disobeying God's wishes. The Koran also tells about the lives of Abraham, Joseph, Moses, and other Hebrew leaders, identifying them as prophets like Muhammad. Jesus Christ is included in this list of prophets, although he is presented as a man rather than the Son of God that Christians believe him to be. At the same time, the Koran compares Christ to an angel because both perform God's will on earth.

In addition, the Koran specifically mandates a belief in angels. Sura (chapter) 2, verse 177 of the Koran says that "it is righteousness to believe in Allah and the Last Day [Judgment Day], and the angels and the Book and the messengers." Like Christians, Muslims believe that there will eventually be a day on which individual humans are judged worthy or unworthy. However, Muslims do not believe in bad angels. Instead they believe in evil spirits or demons, called shaytans, and intermediate spirits who can be either good or evil called *jinn*. The Muslim Satan is sometimes considered a *jinni*, although various sects disagree on whether he was always a *jinni* or became a *jinni* after he disobeyed God. He is also sometimes considered a shaytan. Therefore, Satan's Muslim name, Iblis, is derived from the Greek word *diabolos*, which means "devil."

Most Muslims share the Christian view that Satan's disobedience stemmed from too much pride. In the traditional story in the Koran, Iblis refused to bow to the first man, Adam, as

God has commanded him to do and was therefore cast out of Heaven. In a variation on this story put forth by the Sufi sect of Muslims, Iblis refused to bow to Adam not out of pride, but out of his love for God, believing that only God deserved such a sign of obedience. In any case, when Iblis was punished for his refusal, he blamed humans for turning God against him. He then asked God to allow him to take charge of all evil human beings, and God granted his request.

As with Christians, therefore, the Muslim Satan's role is to cause trouble for human beings. Meanwhile, angels have various duties as God's servants, although their main purpose is to act as messengers between God and human beings. To Muslims, angels are spiritual beings but typically take on human form when visiting earth.

## Jungian Psychology

Muslims, Christians, Jews, and Zoroastrians all believe that angels are real beings, although there is some disagreement among them about what angels look like and what angels do. Some people, however, believe that angels are not real but instead are products of human psychology. One such person was Dr. Carl Gustav Jung, a Swiss psychologist and physician who lived from 1875 to 1961. Jung believed that religious imagery was symbolic of certain aspects of human nature. To him, the battle between good and bad angels, for example, was representative of the battle between the good and bad forces or urges within human beings, who create orderly laws yet are often ruled by chaotic passions. He also found a connection between birds and angels as symbols in stories. For example, he thought that the stork, which appears in folklore as the one who delivers babies to their parents, represents the same positive life force that an angel represents.

Many subsequent psychologists have also suggested that the source of angels is the human mind. Moreover, many people who have written about angels have openly admitted that their work came from their imagination rather than from observations of real angels. But the devoutly faithful would argue that such writings were inspired by God and therefore do indeed describe real angels. They believe that studying these descriptive writings, as well as accounts of angel visitations, can bring insights into the nature of God.

# Chapter 2

# What Do Angels Look Like?

Ever since people first began to speak of angels, writers and artists have attempted to identify what angels look like. Some of these people's written descriptions and painted images have depicted angels made of light or fire. Others have shown angels in the guise of human beings—either as ordinary people or as people with halos and/or wings.

## Looking Like People

The angels of the Old Testament are most commonly said to look like people with no unusual attributes. In this way, angel expert Sophy Burnham suggests in her book *A Book of Angels*, angels are like the spirits worshiped by Native Americans, who often appeared on earth in ordinary human form. She says:

> In the Bible the first angels were men. They came like the [spirit] guides or "familiars" of the American Indians, to walk a few miles beside a hungering human or to help a man or woman at a task. Three [or two with God, according to some scholars] came to Abraham, we are told in Genesis, when Abraham had his tent by the oaks of Mamre.

. . . They had no wings, no shining garments, no halos around their heads. They were three ordinary-looking men, sitting under the oaks, while their host washed their feet with water and served them veal and bread [or cakes of meal] and cheese [or curds]. Moreover, unlike later angels, "they did eat."[2]

Islamic sources also describe some angels as being humanlike in appearance. However, these angels are of monumental size and therefore cannot be mistaken for a human being. For example, in speaking about his encounter with the angel Gabriel, Muhammad said:

*Angels vary greatly in appearance. Some angels appear in a human form.*

When I was midway on the mountain, I heard a voice from heaven saying: "O Muhammad! thou art the apostle of God and I am Gabriel." I raised my head towards heaven to see who was speaking, and lo, Gabriel in the form of a man with feet astride the horizon. . . . I stood gazing at him, moving neither backward or forward; then I began to turn my face away from him, but towards whatever region of the sky I looked, I saw him as before.[3]

## Changing Images

The image of a towering male angel in human form was common in medieval Christian art as well. He was usually clothed in a long, white garment. Some scholars believe that this garment was meant to symbolize the angels' association both with the clouds of heaven and with purity. Others say that white was meant to represent the fact that angels are made of light. Still others, though, say that the white garments were inspired by the white togas worn by Roman senators and therefore represent power and dignity. The fact that medieval angels were sometimes depicted with other symbols of political power, such as a scepter, has been used to support this view; however, a scepter could also be a symbol of God's rule over humans.

During the Renaissance, the image of a huge angel in white garments was gradually replaced by that of a human-sized angel, appearing not only in human form but also in everyday human clothing or, if they were warrior angels, in the traditional armor of knights. Artists also increasingly depicted angels engaging in ordinary human pursuits, to deliberately emphasize their similarity to human beings. As James Underhill, in his book *Angels*, explains:

The medieval image of an angel was a stern, monumental figure clothed in white. Early in the Renaissance a change in costume becomes evident.

*Medieval images of angels were often depicted playing a musical instrument.*

Angels are now seen dressed in rich, heavy garments, with jeweled clasps—regal dress by all means, but of the earth. Their relative size is reduced to a human scale. They are painted playing instruments or singing in choirs [in heaven] closely resembling the performance practices of the time. In short, they become humanized.[4]

But although humanized, Renaissance angels were typically given the most perfect human form that an artist could create. In fact, according to James Underhill, during the Renaissance, "artists used the figure of the angel to express their most exalted conceptions of beauty."[5] If they were shown playing the harp—their most common choice of musical instrument, according to some artists—then their harp was also the most beautiful that the artist could depict.

## Gender

One of the most famous of the Renaissance artists who featured angels in their work was Michelangelo, who lived in Italy from 1475 to 1564. He painted a series of biblical scenes on the ceiling of the Sistine Chapel in Rome, Italy. Several of these scenes feature angels. For example, in *The Last Judgment*, angels are judging human beings and sending them to either Heaven or Hell. Most of the angels, which wear no clothes, are male and have completely normal human forms. According to Michela Zonta and Leonard Day in *Angels A to Z,* "Michelangelo chose this type of visual to show the close association that angels have with man."[6]

In fact, whenever the Bible does mention an angel's gender, it is male. Therefore, medieval Christians—who did not believe in going against whatever the Bible said—always depicted angels as male and often with beards. But during the Renaissance, artists began to show angels as females, and by the end of the period, this was the more common gender in portrayals of angels in art. Even angels like Gabriel, who had a masculine name and was specifically called a male in the Bible, were sometimes shown as female.

Some people have suggested that this change in gender was made because of artists' beliefs on the beauty of the human form. In the Renaissance, as today, many people believe that females are more beautiful than males; therefore, angels like Gabriel, who were supposed to represent the ultimate in beauty, were painted as female. But in his book *Angels,* James Underhill suggests that Gabriel's gen-

*In Michelangelo's painting* The Last Judgment, *the angel depicted resembles a male human.*

der was changed because Renaissance people were uncomfortable with the idea that a male angel would have appeared in the bedroom of a woman, Mary. (Gabriel was the angel who told Mary that she would give birth to Jesus Christ.) Underhill believes that the transformation of other Renaissance angels from male into female was due to similar discomfort over sexual issues. He also notes that Renaissance art frequently features angels as babies who are too young to have any sexual interests.

These baby angels, called cherubs, appear in Michelangelo's Sistine Chapel artwork, and they are present in the works of many other Renaissance artists as well. For example, in the painting *The Nymph Galatea* by the Italian artist Raphael, who lived from 1483 to 1520, the sky is filled with naked male cherubs who are shooting arrows at women below. Raphael's adult angels usually do not seem to have a gender at all.

Modern artists also tend to depict angels as genderless or as female, and like their Renaissance counterparts, their angels are usually very beautiful. Modern writers and filmmakers, however, show angels of both genders, and these angels are far from perfect physically. The 1946 movie *It's a Wonderful Life*, for example, features an angel, named Clarence, who is an overweight older man. The 1996 movie *Michael* also features an overweight angel.

## Wings

In both of these movies, the angels have white wings, although the people around them do not always see these wings. Wings are not a recent addition to angel images. The earliest winged angel in Christian art appears in a fifth-century mosaic in a Roman church. From this point on, wings gradually became a standard feature in portrayals of angels in art.

There are various opinions regarding why people started adding wings to angels. Some scholars believe it was because the first Christian artists to paint and carve angels were inspired by pagan images, particularly those related to Greek and Roman gods. One such image was a goddess of victory called Nike by the Greeks and Victoria by the Romans. In Greek and Roman art, she is portrayed as a human with large wings, usually flying above a triumphant warrior or athlete. Many scholars believe, therefore, that early Christians saw Nike/Victoria as the perfect image to represent the angels who accompanied Christ, whom they also viewed as a triumphant warrior. Rabbi Jay Stevenson explains:

> The view of angels as winged beings isn't obvious from the Bible. In fact, only a very few of the many angels mentioned in scripture are actually said to have wings or fly. . . . Roman Christians adopted the winged victory as a symbol that fused many ideas. Constantine [the emperor of Rome at the time that Christianity became legal] believed that Christ helped him win decisive battles for the struggling Roman Empire, and the winged victory stood in part for the military triumph over pagan foes. The winged figure also stood for the triumph of Christ over evil. Finally, the winged victory symbolized the triumph of life over death.[7]

Other people, however, believe that the inspiration for wings did come from the Bible rather than from pagan sources—because, as even Rabbi Stevenson notes, there are at least a few winged angels in the Bible. One such angel is of a group called *seraphim*—a word which means "fiery beings." According to the Bible, the Hebrew prophet Isaiah saw seraphim in a vision. Isaiah 6:1–3 says:

I saw also the Lord sitting upon a throne, high and lifted up, and his train filled the temple. Above it stood the seraphims: each one had six wings; with twain [two wings] he covered his face, and with twain he covered his feet, and with twain he did fly. And one cried unto another, and said, Holy, holy, holy, *is* the LORD of hosts: the whole earth *is* full of his glory.

Still other scholars say that birds were the inspiration for the wings in artwork portraying angels. For example, Michela Zonta, in *Angels A to Z*, says that "wings were used not only by Christian artists but also by the artists of ancient Egypt, Babylon, Nineveh, and Etruria as symbols of might, majesty, and divine beauty" specifically because of their association with birds. She explains:

Why bird wings should have been taken to represent the spirit is not difficult to understand. To the ancients, birds must have been viewed as marvelous creatures—animals who could shake themselves loose from the earth and float aloft in the invisible medium of the air, an environment much like that of the spirit world. It is but a short step from seeing winged animals as travelers of the air to imagining winged angels as travelers of the spirit realm.[9]

## The Ability to Fly

But regardless of why artists added wings to angels, once they began to do so, they clearly decided that not just any wings would do. Because the angels who served God were perfect beings, artists used the most glorious wings they could find as inspiration for their drawings. At the same time, they used the most ugly wings they could find for depictions of angels who opposed God and served Satan. As Malcolm Godwin explains in his book *Angels: An Endangered Species:*

Largely speaking, the wings chosen to be the most befitting for an angelic body were of course modeled upon the largest and most beautiful birds which were available to the artists for study. Thus it was that the wings of swans, eagles and geese . . . adorned the shoulders of the celestial bodies in the great masterpieces. . . . The hideous denizens of the abyss [Hell], by contrast, were given the wings of reptiles or bats. . . .[10]

However, Godwin points out that there was one problem with either type of wing: It wouldn't be able to lift a human being. He says: "If we examine the anatomical reality of welding wings to earthly form, we find that none of these renderings could possibly fly, yet somehow we have all suspended our disbelief in accepting their possible reality."[11] He explains that according to the laws of physics and gravity, in order for a 200-pound humanlike angel to fly, its wingspan would have to be at least 36 feet and possibly 120 feet. In contrast, the most common wingspan depicted in angel paintings is only about 12 feet.

Nonetheless, Godwin says that most artists who portrayed angels successfully created the illusion that angels can really fly. He says: "The visual trick which has been offered is that they *look* real and yet, without divine and supernatural intervention profoundly adjusting the laws of gravity, we all intuit that these beings could never lift off the ground."[12]

In a few cases, however, artists have not attempted to make the wings look real. Instead, they have used unreal-looking wings to emphasize the otherworldly aspects of angels. For example, some artists have painted angels with flaming wings, while others have shown wings that are made wholly or partly of clouds.

## Halos, Light, and Color

In addition to wings, another common feature of Renaissance angels was halos. These circles of gold and/or white, which sometimes had rays emanating from them, were first associated with angels during the fourth century. As with wings, some scholars believe that halos have their origin in pagan artwork. In some of this artwork, circles of

*In the fourth century, angels first appeared with halos, symbols of light and power.*

gold were used to represent the sun, a symbol of light and power. Since early Christians viewed angels as beings of light and power, these scholars argue, it was natural for them to associate angels with sun disks.

But regardless of its inspiration, the halo in Christian artwork is intended to represent light. People who claim to have seen angels often say that these beings radiate light. For example, Joseph Smith, the founder of the Mormon religion, described the angel Moroni in the book *Essentials of Church History* by saying:

> He had on a loose robe of most exquisite whiteness. It was a whiteness beyond anything earthly I had ever seen; nor do I believe that any earthly thing could be made to appear so exceedingly white and brilliant. His hands were naked, and his arms also, a little above the wrists; so, also, were his feet naked, as were his legs, a little above the ankles. His head and neck were also bare. . . . Not only was his robe exceedingly white, but his whole person was glorious beyond description, and his countenance truly like lightning. The room was exceedingly light, but not so very bright as immediately around his person.[13]

Smith emphasizes that the angel was wearing the color white; other people have associated angels with different colors. For example, in their book *Angels A to Z*, James R. Lewis and Evelyn Dorothy Oliver report:

> It is often stated that when an angel descends to the earth, it brings with it a part of the light of the heavens, thus perhaps explaining the strong association of white to represent that light. Others who have had a close association or visitation with a stronger angelic presence associate specific colors to the entire form. Many identify the color green with

[the angel] Raphael, perhaps to associate the healing of the earth [because Raphael, whose name means "God has healed," is said to be a healer in the *Books of Enoch*]; gold is widely connected with [the angel] Gabriel, perhaps to draw emphasis on his divine messages; Michael is often portrayed in shades of blue to show his protection and solidarity to the heavens, and perhaps in reference to the peacock feathers usually associated with this figure.[14]

But some people believe that angels are of a frequency in the electromagnetic spectrum that cannot be seen with the human eye. According to this theory, angels become visible to humans only when they intentionally change the type of light they emanate in order to enable humans to see them. A related theory suggests that angels glow because they are made of energy but have the ability to appear solid for a short period of time. Still another theory proposes that angels have physical bodies but move at too fast a speed for the human eye to detect; to be seen, an angel must make an effort to slow down.

In discussing such speculations, Eileen Freeman argues that they are not far-fetched, given what people know about the progress of modern science. She explains:

> Until quite recently, the existence of physical bodies we cannot see with our eyes would have been deemed heresy in many parts of the world. When epidemics of plague or typhoid or other diseases swept away the populations of town and cities, no one dreamed that the cause could be a life form with a microscopically small body, too small for anyone to even know the existence of. No one suspected that all matter was made up of infinitesimally small bits of matter called atoms, or that these atoms were made of even smaller bits. Even today, modern science is still discovering new subatomic

particles. . . . We acknowledge that there are life forms we cannot see with our eyes; why shouldn't angels be another life form of this nature, immensely older, wiser, more loving?[15]

## Fiery Angels

But whereas some people associate angels with light, color, and speed, others believe that angels are best represented by a blazing fire. In fact, some passages of the Bible associate angels with fire. The seraphim who visited Isaiah, for example, used fire to purify his lips so that he might later deliver God's words to the people of Israel in pure form without profanity. In Isaiah 6:4, 5-7, the prophet says:

> . . . and the house was filled with smoke. . . . Then flew one of the seraphims unto me, having a live coal in his hand, *which* he had taken with the tongs from off the altar: And he laid *it* upon my mouth, and said, Lo, this hath touched thy lips; and thine iniquity is taken away, and thy sin purged.

Because of their connection to fire, seraphim are typically depicted wearing red, with three pairs of wings and four heads. Some people believe that each head represents a different direction on the compass—north, south, east, and west—while others believe that there are only four seraphim and that each one of them represents a different compass direction.

Another example of an angel with four faces, also connected with fire, is one that appeared to the Hebrew prophet Ezekiel. He had a vision of winged angels emerging from a cloud of flames just prior to the appearance of God himself. In Ezekiel 1:4-6, the prophet says:

> And I looked, and, behold, a whirlwind came out of the north, a great cloud, and a fire infolding itself, and a brightness *was* about it. . . . Also out of the

midst thereof *came* the likeness of four living creatures. And this *was* their appearance; they had the likeness of a man. And every one had four faces, and every one had four wings.

Ezekiel describes the angels' four faces, saying that each angel had the face of a man, the face of a lion, the face of an ox, and the face of an eagle. They had the hands of a man, but the soles of their feet were like those of a calf. They also radiated light. In Ezekiel 1:13, the prophet says:

As for the likeness of the living creatures, their appearance was like burning coals of fire, *and* like the appearance of lamps: it went up and down among the living creatures; and the fire was bright, and out of the fire went forth lightning.

Ezekiel's angels were accompanied by wheels that moved as they moved, seemingly powered by the angels' spirits. Each of these wheels had several eyes. Many scholars believe that these wheels were part of God's chariot, particularly because God's throne—with God seated upon it—appeared to Ezekiel right above the wheels. The association between angels and God's chariot is also apparent in the Old Testament story of Elijah, a prophet who ascended to Heaven in a flaming chariot and, in later Jewish tradition, became an angel himself.

## Bad Angels

But although some good angels are associated with fire, fire has more typically been connected with bad angels throughout history. Satan and his followers are said to live in Hell, which is a place of fire, while God and his angels live in Heaven, a place of light. For this reason, artists such as William Blake (1757–1827), in an illustration for his book *The Marriage of Heaven and Hell*, shows good angels living in light and bad angels in fire.

Bad angels also have a different appearance from good angels, although this was not the case in the earliest artwork depicting angels. For example, in the first Christian art portraying angels, Satan was depicted as a glorious creature—a typically beautiful, humanlike angel with twelve wings. Gradually, however, he became grotesque and took on animal attributes, namely, horns and hooves. Many scholars believe that these animal traits were drawn from gods in pagan religions. For example, Howard Chua-Eoan says:

As late as the sixth century A.D. . . . the devil was
still portrayed as a haloed, winged being, standing
at the left hand of Christ. Satan is dressed in blue,
not red, robes. (Red was the color of the upper
ether [the region of space above the air], closest to
God, from which Satan was expelled; blue the color
of the closest heaven humankind could see.) By the
Middle Ages, however, Satan had become a beast.
His horns and hooves come from his commingling
with beliefs banished by a victorious Christianity.
The devil's appurtenances derive from the great
Greek god Pan—half-man, half-goat—and from
association with the cult of the forest deity
Cernunnos of northern Europe. Relegated to the
shadows, the pagan gods were absorbed by the
master of darkness, the demigod on the margins
[Satan].[16]

In other words, Satan became associated with religions
that the Christians considered bad—pagan religions, which
featured gods that often looked either partly or wholly animal. But, interestingly, while Chua-Eoan says that Satan
was originally colored blue to designate his separation from
God, who was associated with the color red, today red is the
color most commonly associated with Satan. It is unclear
how this association originated; however, since it occurred
during a time when people were rejecting monarchies, some
scholars speculate that it developed because red was the traditional color of royalty. Also, it may have developed from
the popular idea of Hell as a place of fire.

In any case, Satan is often depicted in artwork with red
skin, red horns, and a red forked tail. This fork is probably
meant to suggest a connection between Satan and snakes,
which have forked tongues; it was a snake who tempted
Eve to disobey God, thereby causing her to be cast out of
the Garden of Eden. Satan's wings, when they are depicted,

are those of a bat or a dragon, two creatures—one real, one imaginary—that early Christians considered evil.

Up until modern times, although Satan was depicted as having some animal characteristics—horns and a tail—he still had the basic appearance of a human. But today's Satan, as he is shown in popular movies and television programs, is sometimes depicted as a horrific monster with reptilian features. Alternatively, he is shown in ordinary human form. Considered a master of disguise, he typically pretends to be a human—either male or female—in order to tempt human beings to sin. For example, in one episode

*Bad angels are often depicted as humans with animal characteristics such as horns, hooves, and batlike wings.*

of the television show *Touched by an Angel,* Satan is a man who forms a racist group and urges people to commit hate crimes. In another, Satan is a woman whose intent is to convince someone to sell his soul to Satan so that his wife can afford an expensive medical treatment. The idea of giving Satan a soul in exchange for riches is also part of the premise of the 2000 movie *Bedazzled* (a remake of a 1967 movie), which features a female Satan who offers a man seven wishes in exchange for his soul.

But even when Satan appears in human form, his true form is always a glimmer beneath the surface. In many popular television shows and movies in which Satan is pretending to be human, his eyes occasionally revert to those of a reptile. Few modern people imagine that Satan might always look the same as any other person or might be as beautiful as any angel. This is a holdover from medieval times, when people firmly believed that the appearance of a person always reflected his or her character. In other words, most bad people were ugly and vice versa; most good people were beautiful and vice versa. This concept influenced the way that ideas developed about how good and bad angels behave. People's views about angel behavior have traditionally been closely related to their views about good and bad angels' appearances.

# What Do Good Angels Do?

G ood angels are distinguished from bad ones by virtue of the fact that they serve God, whereas bad angels—now traditionally called demons or devils—serve Satan. However, many authors have gone beyond simply saying that angels do whatever God wants. Their writings have attempted to assign specific duties to specific types of angels, to identify how much time each type of angel spends on earth, and to describe the angels' realm in Heaven.

## Describing Heaven

In modern times, Heaven is often referred to as a place of light and love. Sometimes, it is depicted as a paradise, a perfect garden with the most beautiful scenery imaginable. At other times, it is described as just like earth, only better. For example, one popular nineteenth-century American novelist, Elizabeth Stuart Phelps Ward, wrote a series of books—the first of which was *The Gates Ajar* (1869)—that depicted Heaven as a utopian society with houses and activities more perfect than any ever created by human beings. More commonly, however, authors have presented the afterlife as a strange, awe-inspiring, sometimes frightening place that is difficult for the human mind to comprehend. This was the case with Richard Matheson's 1978 book and 1998 movie *What Dreams May Come*, both of which suggested that each person creates his or her own Heaven based on the expectations within that person's imagination.

In earlier times, people's views on Heaven were even more complex. For example, in the eighteenth century, the Swedish scientist and philosopher Emmanuel Swedenborg argued that there are three different Heavens: the celestial Heaven, the spiritual Heaven, and the ultimate Heaven. According to Swedenborg, each Heaven is inhabited by a different type of angel and a different type of human spirit. The celestial Heaven is for those who are perfect enough to communicate directly with God. The spiritual Heaven is for those who are good and kind but imperfect. The ultimate Heaven, which is farthest from God, is for selfish spirits and angels. Evil spirits and angels inhabit Hell, where they are punished for trying to harm others. In writing about Heaven and Hell, Swedenborg said he was inspired by the angels themselves, who he claimed spoke to him on a regular basis.

*Italian philosopher St. Thomas Aquinas believed in angel hierarchies.*

## Angel Hierarchies

Swedenborg was not the first to attempt to categorize angels. There have been many authors who have ranked angels according to both their closeness with God and their duties as God's servants. Perhaps the earliest was Pseudo-Dionysius, whose sixth century writings identified nine choirs or divisions of angels. During the Middle Ages, his works were expanded upon by the Italian philosopher St. Thomas Aquinas, who lived from 1225 to 1274.

Aquinas gave popular lectures that spread the idea of the angel hierarchy throughout the medieval world, and today his ideas are still accepted as truth by many believers in angels. In discussing a lecture that Aquinas gave at the University of Paris in 1259, Sophy Burnham talks about the scholar's popularity both in the Middle Ages and today. She says:

> [During the Middle Ages] great teachers such as . . . Thomas Aquinas attracted tremendous crowds to hear them discourse upon a subject with arguments and counterarguments that involved long quotations from memory of the classics or Scripture and the complex use of logic and reasoning. People came to hear them like spectators at a football game . . . for the sheer admiration of style and clarity of thought. Such talks might even take several days. Thus, Thomas held fifteen discourses on angels over a period of a week, setting out everything known or asked about them and answering the audience's questions. His lectures were written down as he spoke them and formed the foundation of our knowledge about angels for the next eight hundred years.[17]

Like Dionysius, Aquinas identified nine choirs of angels arranged in a hierarchy with the least powerful at the bottom and the most powerful at the top. The duties of an angel and the amount of time that that angel will spend on earth are defined by the angel's position in the hierarchy. Aquinas also divided his angels into three groups, with three choirs in each. The highest triad of the three, the one that spends the most time in communion with God and has the most power and responsibility, is known as the Angels of Pure Contemplation (or, in some interpretations of Aquinas's work, the Angels of Pure Goodness). The middle triad is the Angels of the Cosmos, so named because they spend most of their time governing the universe in the realm between God and man. The third and lowest triad is the Angels of the World, so named because they spend most of their time on earth.

## Angels of Pure Contemplation

The angels that make up the Angels of Pure Contemplation are—in descending order of power and authority—the seraphim, the cherubim, and the thrones. As a group, they govern all creation. They are also the most radiant of all angels, as well as the most difficult for humans to comprehend. As Janice Connell says: "Their holiness is so intense that the human mind is incapable of comprehending their levels of adoration and participation in the Divinity."[18]

Seraphim are charged with guarding God's throne and wield flaming swords to enforce God's will. They continuously chant "Holy, Holy, Holy is the Lord of Hosts, the whole earth is full of His Glory" in Hebrew.[19] Because they are so close to God, they avoid contact with all other beings except for Christ, the archangel Michael, and the Virgin Mary. Christians who consider Mary the Queen of the Angels believe that when she appears on earth, she is always accompanied by seraphim.

The cherubim are only slightly less powerful than the seraphim. They, too, accompany the Virgin Mary, and their images often adorn temples. Statues of cherubim made of gold are also said to have adorned the Ark of the Covenant, which the Hebrews believed held the tablets of the Ten Commandments. The name cherubim means either "ones who pray" or "ones who intercede." These angels always sit beside God's throne, unless he has sent them to guard some holy place. Like seraphim, cherubim wield flaming swords to enforce God's will.

The lowest members of the triad, the thrones, are also called the Galgallim, from the Hebrew word *galgal,* "wheel." These angels are mentioned in the Old Testament book of Ezekiel as being linked to wheels appearing just below God; consequently, many people have concluded that the thrones are God's living chariots, bearing his throne wherever he wants to go. According to this view, the cherubim who sit beside God are the charioteers. Other people, however, think that the thrones are the charioteers rather than the chariot itself, and some say that these angels are named "thrones" not because they carry God's throne, but because they have a thronelike role in the heavenly hierarchy. Janice Connell explains:

They are named Thrones because the very power of God that emanates to all that is created in the heavens and the cosmos and the earth "rests" upon the Thrones. All the lower Choirs of Angels are dependent upon the Thrones to access God. The Thrones are so filled with humility that God, who presides over them, carries out His Divine Justice through them.[20]

Some Christians believe that God has given the thrones the power to punish human beings. These angels might punish directly, or they might assign another angel the task of punishing a particular individual. Other Christians believe that the thrones are too filled with humility to judge people.

## The Angels of the Cosmos

The choirs of angels within the middle triad, the Angels of the Cosmos, are—again, in descending order—the dominions, the virtues, and the powers. As a group, they receive their power from the Angels of Pure Contemplation; the power radiates outward through that triad from God.

The highest members of the Angels of the Cosmos, the dominions, govern all created matter and supervise the duties of all lesser angels. In doing so, they receive assignments from the thrones. Dominions are concerned with order and discipline, cause and effect. Some people call them the Angels of Leadership, while others call them the Spirits of Wisdom. Four dominions are said to rule over all the rest: Zadkiel, Hashmal, Yahriel, and Muriel.

The virtues, also known as "the shining ones," are the angels in charge of earthly miracles. They help people avoid accidents—unless these accidents lead to great discoveries—and give them courage when heroism is needed. Many people believe that virtues escorted Christ to Heaven after his crucifixion, and some say that virtues were attendants to Eve when she gave birth to Cain. Some people think that Satan was a virtue before he was cast out of Heaven.

Most of the fallen angels, however, came from the next choir of angels, the powers. Interestingly, the powers are responsible for fighting fallen angels and keeping them from trying to get into Heaven, a job which entails much risk. As Malcolm Godwin explains:

> [Powers] appear to act as a kind of border guard who patrol the Heavenly Pathways on the lookout for devilish infiltration. These patrols are obviously a risky business and St. Paul [one of Christ's missionaries] sternly warned his various flocks [followers] that Powers can be both good and evil. In

*Many Christians believe that the virtues, angels in charge of miracles, escorted Christ to Heaven.*

Romans 13:1 [of the New Testament], it is revealed that "The Soul is subject to the Powers," and it is in their efforts to keep a balance within our souls that some are known to become over-identified with the darker side of human beings and thus to fall. Even so the Powers find their true vocation in balancing or reconciling opposites.[21]

## Angels of the World

Aquinas believed that the farther that angels dwelled from God and the more time that they spent around human beings, the more likely it was for them to become bad angels. After all, Satan's servants—the fallen angels—were once good angels who had disobeyed God after being on earth for a while. Moreover, Aquinas theorized, even if an angel didn't become bad because of too much contact with humans, the angel could still become less than perfect. This view remains popular today and is reflected in the movie *Wings of Desire* (remade as *City of Angels* in 1998), in which an angel decides to give up his wings so that he can woo a human woman and enjoy other earthly plea-sures. Similarly, in the 1996 movie *Michael*, an angel is depicted smoking, drinking, and womanizing while he is on earth.

It is because being around humans is so tempting that the powers—who are lowest in the middle triad and there-fore close to earth—are at risk of becoming fallen angels. This is even more true for the angels in the lowest triad, the Angels of the World. In fact, angels depicted in movies as being unable to resist temptation are usually from this third triad.

The three choirs of angels within this triad are, in descending order, the principalities, the archangels, and the angels. The principalities protect large entities, such as religions, towns, cities, and nations. If the people of these places pray for God's help, the principalities are allowed to intervene in human behavior and events within their assigned locations. The archangels also intervene in human events—again, providing that human beings ask for their help—as emissaries for the principalities. Moreover, they deliver God's messages to human beings on earth and command the forces of good against the forces of evil.

According to Islamic faith, there are only four archangels; the Koran names two of them, Michael and Gabriel. Christians and Jews believe that there are seven archangels. The names of three—Michael, Gabriel, and Raphael—are not in dispute, but people disagree on the identity of the remaining four. The archangels Michael and Gabriel are mentioned several times in both the Bible and the Koran, and both archangels are also featured in Jewish and Christian stories.

By all accounts, Michael is a warrior of great power. Many people believe that he personally threw Satan out of Heaven and that he commands all Heavenly warriors in their battles against evil. Some stories give Michael other roles as well. For example, in Jewish tales he sometimes acts as a messenger; in particular, he is said to have been the angel who spoke to Moses from the burning bush. Christian stories sometimes refer to him as the angel responsible for escorting the souls of the newly deceased to Heaven. In the ancient Near East, people sometimes called upon Michael to cure illness. During the Middle Ages, this concept inspired the development of a cult in Western Europe; people worshiped Michael as an angelic healer and made pilgrimages to churches and cathedrals bearing his name. The Catholic Church condemned this practice for a time, but the cult persisted nonetheless.

The archangel Gabriel is the angel of truth in the Islamic faith, but in Judaism and Christianity, Gabriel is the angel of revelation and mercy. Christians believe that

Gabriel appeared to announce the births of both John the Baptist and Jesus Christ, and according to some stories, Gabriel escorts souls from Heaven to human wombs to await birth. In part because of this association with pregnancy, some people have suggested that Gabriel is female, although according to both the Bible and the Koran, Gabriel is male.

The archangel Raphael, whose name means "God has healed," is the angel of healing and is responsible for human diseases and medicine. Also called the angel of science, Raphael is the bringer of knowledge as well. He sometimes acts as a matchmaker and enjoys visiting earth to talk with humans who do not recognize him as an angel.

*Archangel Raphael is both the angel of healing and the angel of science.*

Among the names proposed for the remaining archangels are Uriel, Sammael, Sariel, Raziel, and Metatron. The archangel Uriel is sometimes called the angel of repentance and is responsible for punishing the souls of sinners in the afterlife. By some accounts, Uriel also warns of disaster. For example, he is said to have appeared to Noah to warn him that a great flood would soon cover the earth. Sammael is often said to be the angel of death, Sariel the prince of ministering angels, Raziel the angel of mysteries, and Metatron a heavenly archivist who writes down truths and acts as the main conduit of communication between God and human beings. The Jews see Metatron as perhaps the most important of all angels, whereas to Christians he is a relatively unimportant figure.

Because the archangels have such important responsibilities and are so close to humans, some people do not believe them to be subservient to angels in higher triads. In other words, they believe that these angels have superior powers, even though their primary duties lie on earth rather than in Heaven. According to this view, archangel is a job rather than a choir position; archangels are, therefore, also members of higher choirs and/or in charge of angels in other choirs in addition to holding the job of archangel. Gabriel, for example, is sometimes called the ruler of the cherubim, and Raphael has been variously called a throne, a dominion, a cherub, a power, or the ruler of the virtues. Interestingly, Satan is often said to have been a virtue before his fall, as well as a former archangel.

## Guardian Angels

The lowest choir of good angels, known simply as the angels, is composed of angels whose job is to help individual humans in their daily pursuits. For example, some angels are in charge of inspiring music and invention, while others take care of places on earth that people enjoy visiting, such as gardens, forests, mountains, and rivers.

The angel that has the most contact with individual humans is the guardian angel, whose primary job is to protect a human being throughout that person's life.

The idea of a helpful angel began with stories about the angel Raphael. Raphael first appeared in the Book of Tobit, which is considered deuterocanonical (part of a secondary canon) by Catholics and apocryphal (not part of the canon) by Protestants and Jews. In the *Book of Tobit*, Raphael went to earth specifically to answer the prayers of a man named Tobit, who wanted a wife for his son, Tobias. Raphael—appearing in the guise of an ordinary man—acted as a matchmaker between Tobias and Sarah, a woman who had also prayed for help from God. In subsequent stories, beginning in the ninth century, Raphael brought other lovers together, healed the wounded, and helped people in a variety of ways.

Although Raphael is no longer the focus of angel stories, helpfulness is the most common trait associated with angels in modern literature and film. For example, the television program *Touched by an Angel* features angels who come to earth to help a series of troubled but worthy individuals; this show has also inspired novels about encounters with helpful angels. Similarly, the movie *Angels in the Outfield* (1951, remade in 1994) concerns a team of angels that comes to earth to help a losing baseball team. The angel Clarence in *It's a Wonderful Life* (1946) is a guardian angel who stops a man from committing suicide, and then shows him the positive effect that his life has had on everyone around him. The movie *A Guy Named Joe* (1943), remade as *Always* (1989), concerns the spirit of a man who is assigned to act as a guardian angel to the woman he once loved on earth.

The concept of a guardian angel—who is not just helpful but helpful to one specific individual throughout that individual's life—originated in religious writings. Writings of the Jewish faith, for example, say that every Jew is

*An angel Clarence (Henry Travers, left) is sent to help a desperate George Bailey (James Stewart, right) in the 1946 film* It's a Wonderful Life.

assigned eleven thousand guardian angels on the day that he or she is born. Christians believe that each person is assigned only one guardian angel at birth. However, many Christians also believe that as people become more perfect, they require a larger number of guardian angels to watch out for them, because they are more likely to be tempted by fallen angels. For example, Janice Connell says:

> In the higher realms of spiritual awareness people are guarded by a team of angels. The path is more difficult as the ascent to God continues because the attacks of the rebel spirits are more vicious and cunning. Obviously the stakes are higher. The ministrations of the angelic team defend a soul's

attempts to conform more perfectly to the will of God. This behavior enrages the rebel spirits [Satan's servants], who loathe the will of God.[22]

But, according to Christian belief, most people will never reach the level of spiritual awareness where they need a full team of angels. Instead, they will continue to have just one or two guardian angels throughout their lives. In most cases, these guardian angels act without being seen, but sometimes people claim they have actually met their guardian angels. Reporter Nancy Gibbs describes the typical situation that such people report:

> A person is in immediate danger—the car stalled in the deadly snowstorm, the small plane lost in the fog, the swimmer too far from shore. And emerging from the moment's desperation comes some logical form of rescue: a tow-truck driver, a voice from the radio tower, a lifeguard. But when the victim is safe and turns to give thanks, the rescuer is gone. There are no tire tracks in the snow. There is no controller in the tower. And there are no footprints on the beach.[23]

It is only after such an encounter that the person decides that the helper has been a guardian angel rather than another human being.

In some cases, however, guardian angels do identify themselves during the encounter. Gibbs relates two such stories. In the first, an angel appeared to a woman with cancer, said that he was sent by God, and announced that her cancer was cured. The woman passed out, and when she woke up, the angel was gone—and so was her cancer, according to doctors who subsequently examined her. In the second story, a man in the hospital was visited by his guardian angel, who brought words of comfort from God. When the man told his wife of this visitation, it was clear he was at peace, and he remained so until his death two days later.

## The Angels of Mons

There have also been reports of angels appearing to help large groups of people. Perhaps the best known of these is an incident that occurred on a World War I battlefield near Mons, Belgium, in August 1914. French and British allied soldiers were fighting against an advancing German army, and it looked as though the Germans would win. Then the tide of battle turned; fire from the allies suddenly increased, and the Germans retreated. At first this seemed to be a normal battlefield event. But wounded French and British soldiers told an unusual tale while in the hospital. They insisted that they had not been fighting alone; they had seen angels on the battlefield fighting with them.

French soldiers said that the army of angels had been led by the archangel Michael. British soldiers said the angelic general was St. George, known for slaying dragons. A few said there were only a few angels, while most saw many. Descriptions of the angels also varied, although most of the soldiers said they emanated a bright light and had wings.

At first such remarks were dismissed as being due to the soldiers' poor health. But soon public opinion of the event changed. Nancy Gibbs explains why:

> Some soldiers later speculated that their exhaustion had brought on hallucinations. Others thought it was mass hysteria, the result of a battle that was supposed to be easily won by the allies but had turned into a rout. But later stories emerged from the German side of the same incident. The Kaiser's soldiers said they found themselves "absolutely powerless to proceed . . . and their horses turned around sharply and fled." The Germans said the allied position was held by thousands of troops—though in fact there were only two regiments there.[24]

*Belgian, British, and French soldiers were convinced that angels helped them in a World War I battle with the Germans.*

Over the years, various explanations have been proposed for why the German reports seemed to support the stories of their enemies. Some people blame the heat of battle for distorting all of the soldiers' perception of events. Moreover, skeptics often say that the explanation for the Angels of Mons, as they are commonly called, lies in a short story, "The Bowmen" by Arthur Machen, that was published near the beginning of the war. Machen told of an army of angels that came to the rescue of British troops, and there are many similarities between his angels and the Angels of Mons. But Machen's story was published in September 1914, three weeks *after* the Mons event occurred. Consequently, the majority of people who know about the incident at Mons accept as a fact the idea that angels appeared to the soldiers there.

A few, however, protest that angels would never be so unfair as to appear selectively to human beings. For example, playwright Tony Kushner, the author of *Angels in America*, has complained about the belief that angels show up to help some human beings and not others. He says:

> I find that [idea] horribly offensive. The question is, why are you saved with your guardian angel and not the woman who was shot to death shielding her children in Brooklyn three weeks ago? That suggests a capricious divine force. If there is a God, he can't possibly work that way.[25]

Some believers in angels address this complaint by saying that good angels are not always able to counter the effects of Satan and his servants, who cause such events as shootings to occur. To these people, the existence of devils explains much of what is wrong with the world, and the existence of good angels much of what is right with the world. Good angels work to create order, devils to create chaos—and people are free to choose which path to follow.

# Chapter 4

# Devils: What Do Bad Angels Do?

According to most people's beliefs, when angels first came into being, they were all good. Then some of them disobeyed God and were cast out of Heaven. These "fallen angels," sometimes called bad angels but more commonly referred to as devils or demons, behave very differently from good angels, and they live in a very different place from Heaven.

## Angels of Punishment

The earliest Christians believed that good angels called the Angels of Punishment and the Angels of Destruction were responsible for punishing humans after death and causing destruction on earth in accordance with God's will. Their belief was based on Jewish writings that suggested that the Hebrew leader Moses encountered five punishing angels in Hell: Af, the angel of anger; Kezef, the angel of wrath; Hemah, the angel of fury; Hasmed, the angel of annihilation; and Mashit, the angel of destruction. These angels were considered so fierce and so eager to inflict serious punishments that Malcolm Godwin says, "With such righteous angels of the Lord hacking away at the wretched sinners, one marvels at the need of Devils at all."[26]

But early Christians soon became uncomfortable with the idea of such fierce and punishing good angels, so they gave the job of punishing sinners to devils. The word *devil* comes from the Greek word *diabolos*, which means "slanderer," and it has long been associated with evil. The other word used for the fallen angels, *demon*, comes from the Greek word *daimon*, or "spirit," and was originally used to refer to both good and bad spirits; the early Christians of Rome, however, decided that all demons were bad.

*Angels cast out of Heaven are known as bad angels, fallen angels, devils, or demons.*

During the Middle Ages, when St. Thomas Aquinas was lecturing on hierarchies of good angels, people were also discussing the duties of devils. Some felt that every good angel had to have a corresponding bad angel—just as in the Zoroastrian religion, the good god Ahura Mazda has an evil counterpart, Angra Mainyu. Their view was that the hierarchy of angels in Hell was exactly like the hierarchy of angels in Heaven. Other people felt that Hell, which is a place of chaos, would not have such an organized hierarchy. However, they did accept the idea that, like good angels, devils would fall into broad categories according to how much time they spent on earth and how close they were to their leader, Satan.

## Types of Devils

According to this view, the devils with the most contact with humans are called simply that: devils. They cause mischief for individual human beings, much as guardian angels protect individual human beings. Demons are a similar type of creature, but they create general chaos among human beings as a whole.

Other fallen angels spend all of their time in Hell and, therefore, have contact only with bad humans who have died, if they have any contact with them at all. These include Xaphan, who keeps the furnaces running in Hell so that it is constantly fiery; and Dommiel, who is in charge of the gates of Hell but, unlike St. Peter—who is said to guard the gates of Heaven—refuses entrance to no one. Two other significant angels in Hell are Beleth and Crocell, who before their fall were good angels in the powers category. They command huge armies of devils in Hell, preparing them for the day when good and bad angels will battle.

Still another angel in Hell is Apollyon, also called Abbadon, whose name means "destroyer." He is in charge of a bottomless pit in Hell that is inhabited by insects with human faces. In ancient times he sometimes let these

*This sculpture by Auguste Rodin depicts the gates of Hell.*

insects loose to plague mankind. According to some stories, Apollyon also once trapped Satan in the bottomless pit and kept him there for a thousand years. For this reason, early Christians considered Apollyon a good angel who trapped Satan in order to keep the devil away from human beings. In modern times, however, it is generally believed that Apollyon is a bad angel who trapped Satan not to protect mankind, but so that he could rule Hell himself.

## The Princes of Hell

Supervising all the angels in Hell are the Princes of Hell, who are closest to Satan and, before the fall, were once the most powerful angels in Heaven. The Princes of Hell include Baal-berith, Mephistopheles, and Rofocale. Once a cherub in Heaven, Baal-berith oversees contracts made with humans who want to sell their soul to Satan in exchange for some earthly pleasure. Baal-berith is also in charge of all official events in Hell; in other words, when devils meet to make plans, Baal-berith runs the meeting unless Satan is present. Mephistopheles, who was once an archangel in Heaven, often acts as a substitute for Satan in evil dealings on earth. Rofocale also might have been an archangel, although his former position in Heaven is in dispute. In Hell, however, he is clearly the prime minister. He influences the distribution of monetary wealth among humans, since poverty sometimes tempts people to rob, steal, or cheat.

Another significant Prince of Hell is Beelzebub, also called Baal the Prince. Modern Christians believe that Beelzebub and Satan are the same devil. However, in ancient times Beelzebub and Satan, who were mentioned separately in both the Old Testament and the New, were thought of as two distinct beings. Ancient Hebrews gave Beelzebub a name meaning "Lord of the Flies," while some early Christians thought he was in charge of the devils who sometimes took over, or possessed, the bodies of human beings on earth. The latter belief stems from the fact that in the New Testament, Luke 11:14–15 says of Jesus Christ:

> And he was casting out a devil [from someone's body], and it was dumb. And it came to pass, when the devil was gone out . . . [some people said] He casteth out devils through Beelzebub the chief of the devils.

Today, stories continue to be told of devils taking over control of a person's body. Known as *demonic possession*, this phenomenon is considered a psychological illness by people who do not believe in angels. Believers, however, generally accept the possibility that one of Satan's agents can take over the soul of a person before that person is dead. Someone who is possessed might curse, perform disgusting and/or evil deeds, and display violent body movements. One of the most popular fictionalized accounts of demonic possession is *The Exorcist* by William Peter Blatty, a 1971 novel and 1973 movie that was loosely based on a real-life case of demonic possession in Washington D.C., reported in newspapers. In Blatty's story, the possessing devil is said to be a lesser demon, rather than Satan or Beelzebub.

Interestingly, Beelzebub's name is the same as that of a pagan Phoenecian god once worshiped in Israel. There are also numerous archangels, dukes, and arch-she-demons of Hell that have the same names and/or defining characteristics as those belonging to pagan gods and goddesses. Scholars believe that this practice was a way for early Zoroastrians, Hebrews, and Christians to demonize the pagan gods that they had rejected. For example, the arch-she-demon Proserpine has the name of a Roman goddess and shares many traits with the goddess Kali of India, and the arch-she-demon Astarte has the name of a Phoenician goddess and is much like the Egyptian goddess Hathor. Both of these arch-she-demons were forces of destruction. Similarly, in identifying which angels fell from God's grace, early Christians often chose ones that were said to have watched over rival nations. For example, one of the archangels of Hell is Dubbiel, who appears in early Hebrew stories as the guardian angel of Persia.

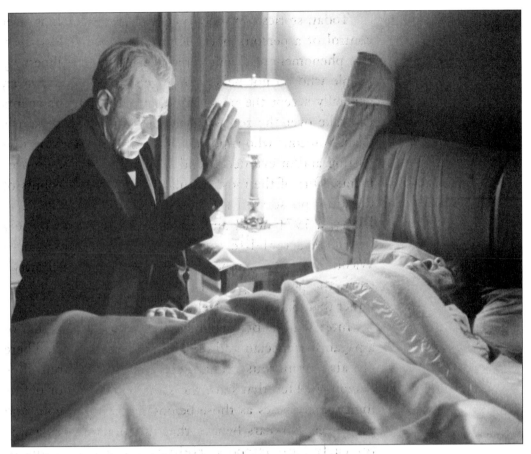

## The Fall

The leader of the fallen angels, Satan, was once a loyal follower of God. There are many stories of how Satan—who some believe was called Lucifer before his fall—turned bad. One of the most dramatic of these stories involves the concept of free will, by which individuals are free to make their own choices in life. According to this story, after God created angels—but, in most versions of the story, before he created human beings—he suspected that giving them free will would make them disobedient. He decided, therefore, to give only half of his angels free will. Within a short time, the group with free will—led by Satan—began to engage in wrong behavior.

*Actor Max von Sydow performs an exorcism on actress Linda Blair in the popular 1973 film,* The Exorcist.

A variation of this story has God giving both groups free will, with only one choosing to embrace evil, whereupon a huge battle broke out between the good and bad angels. There are various accounts of how this battle progressed; many feature the archangel Michael personally throwing Satan out of Heaven. All the accounts featuring a battle in Heaven, however, suggest that the stories of fallen angels who became bad by misbehaving on earth are incorrect. But in modern times, a few religious leaders have suggested that there are two types of fallen angels, those who sinned on earth and those who fought the battle in Heaven. According to this scenario, the warrior angels have more responsibilities and power in Hell than the angels who committed earthly sins. In a variation on this scenario, the angels who committed earthly sins were transformed into human beings who lived on earth; their descendants are the most evil people living today.

But regardless of different versions, almost all stories about fallen angels suggest that they were responsible for their own fall. This is in accordance with the belief in most faiths that people are ultimately responsible for choosing right or wrong. However, Hindus believe that one of the defining qualities of demons is their inability to judge right from wrong. Therefore, in the Hindu faith, demons are considered blameless for their actions.

## Where Devils Live

However, according to the prevailing Christian view, devils not only know right from wrong but also are determined to get human beings to make wrong choices. To this end, Satan himself typically takes on human form to visit earth and tempt people to become his followers. Some people believe that Satan travels back and forth between earth and Hell, but others think that Satan spends all of his time on earth. For example, in *The Political History of the Devil* published in 1726, Daniel Defoe says:

Satan, being thus confined to a vaga-bond, wandering, unsettled condition, is without any certain abode; for though he has, in consequence of his angelic nature, a kind of empire in the liquid waste or air, yet this is certain-ly part of his punish-ment, that he is . . . without any fixed place, or space, allowed him to rest the sole of his foot upon.[27]

Still other people believe that Satan cannot leave Hell at all. In this view, the angels of Hell can punish only the souls of people who, with free will like the angels themselves, have chosen to sin without being tricked into it and therefore ended up in Hell by their own doing.

Most people agree that once in Hell, bad people are punished by devils or demons. But people disagree on where this place is located. The prevailing Christian view is that it is either deep within the hottest regions of the earth or on a spiritual plane far below Heaven yet not on earth. In either case, Hell is physically and spiritually dis-tant from God.

A sixteenth-century painting by Raphael portrays the archangel Michael forcing Satan out of Heaven.

The idea that Hell is a separate region from Heaven is different from the view established by the Hebrews, who believed that there were places of Hellish punishment in various parts of Heaven. The Hebrews proposed that there are seven layers of Heaven, with the highest being in the stars and the lowest nearest the earth, where the clouds and winds are formed. They believe that each layer has its own ruling angel, as well as many other angels in charge of various aspects of each heaven. Below these seven layers of Heaven are seven layers of earth, each with different landscapes, climates, and inhabitants. All of these layers—both of Heaven and of Hell—are linked together by massive hooks.

*Many people believe that sinners are sent to Hell and punished.*

The world we know is the central point of this system, in between the lowest level of Heaven and the highest level of earth. Moreover, according to some Hebrew stories, in addition to the Hellish places that exist in each level of Heaven, a Hell exists in the sixth layer of earth specifically to house the angels, and this Hell, too, has seven layers. This Hell is known as Gehenna, and Malcolm Godwin describes it as being "sixty times as big as our earth. Each of its palaces has six thousand houses, each with six thousand vessels of fire and gall for the unfortunate sinner."[28]

Once in Hell, people are sent to one region or another in accordance with what type of punishment they deserve. However, Jews and Christians disagree on whether sinners are punished in Hell just for a little while or forever. Jews believe the former, while Christians believe the latter. However, Christians also believe that people who repent their sins deserve a second chance. Therefore, some Christians think that there is a prisonlike region, within Hell or separate from Hell, called Purgatory, where repentant sinners "serve time" before going to Heaven. The amount of time served depends on the severity of the sins committed and the degree of repentance expressed. While in Purgatory, former sinners pray, cry, and eat only bread and water.

## An Escort to the Afterlife

Most Christians further believe that the souls of the deceased are led to Heaven, Purgatory, or Hell by angels called psychopomps—a word that means "soul guides" in Greek and was originally applied to the Greek god Hermes, who conducted souls to the underworld—or by the angel of death. These angels serve God but are in a class separate from the good angels. Their contact with Hell does not place them at risk of becoming a fallen angel; they are immune to Hell's temptations, concentrating only on their escort duties.

In the television show *Touched by an Angel*, which primarily reflects Christian beliefs, the angel of death is portrayed as a handsome young man, named Andrew, who helps people die peacefully. Jews, however, view the angel of death as a frightening figure, while Muslims see the angel of death—Azrael—as being helpful only to true believers in the Islamic faith. When the Islamic angel of death comes to Muslims, he eases their souls gently from their bodies and sends them to Heaven, but when he comes to nonbelievers, he yanks their souls roughly from their bodies and casts them into Hell. Muslims further believe that the angel of death knows when someone is not a true believer because other angels have been recording people's prayers and can testify either for or against any individual's worthiness to enter Heaven.

Some Christians, however, do not believe that angels—either good or bad—escort souls to Heaven or Hell after death. Instead, they believe that souls must wait to go anywhere apart from their human body until a final Judgment Day, when angels awaken the dead and judge whether each person is worthy of Heaven. Muslims believe this as well; for them, an angel named Israfel will blow a trumpet to awaken the dead. However, people who believe in Judgment Day disagree on whether people's physical bodies actually arise from the grave, as well as on whether these bodies would appear intact, decomposed, or as they were when the people were young. They also disagree on whether souls wait within bodies for Judgment Day. Some say that they dwell in Purgatory, Paradise—an idyllic spot similar to Heaven but without God's presence—or some other temporary place while awaiting the angels' call to come forth and be judged.

## The Fight for Souls

As part of their belief in Judgment Day, most Christians also believe that good and bad angels will fight a huge battle at the end of the world, similar to the one that they fought at the beginning of the world. According to this view, the fallen angels have been seething for centuries over the loss that they experienced in their first battle with God's angels, and they have been planning to try again to take over Heaven. Some Christians believe that while the climactic battle in Heaven will eventually take place, in the meantime, groups of bad angels are already fighting in skirmishes with groups of good angels. For example, the Rev. Billy Graham says:

*According to some Christians, on Judgment Day angels will awaken the dead and determine whether they will be allowed into Heaven.*

> We live in a perpetual battlefield—the great War of the Ages continues to rage. The lines of battle press

in ever more tightly about God's own people. The wars among nations on earth are merely popgun affairs compared to the fierceness of battle in the spiritual, unseen world. This invisible spiritual conflict is waged around us incessantly and unremittingly. Where the Lord works, Satan's forces hinder; where angel beings carry out their divine directives, the devils rage. All this comes about because the powers of darkness press their counterattack to recapture the ground held for the glory of God.[29]

To many Christians, these skirmishes are manifested in an ongoing struggle for human souls as devils try to entice people to commit evil deeds. To get someone to turn toward evil, a devil will lie, cheat, or do anything else necessary to trick a person into becoming bad. Some Christians believe that a devil can approach anyone at will, while others believe that a devil must first be invited into someone's life in order to cause harm. Usually, this invitation is issued through magic. As Rabbi Jay Stevenson explains:

> Sources disagree in regard to Satan's power over humanity on Earth. Some say Satan and the fallen angels are stuck in hell where they have power only over the lost souls who are condemned to an afterlife of endless torment. Others say that devils walk the earth and interfere in the lives of mortal humans. Somewhere in the middle is the view that devils can appear on Earth only when summoned through black magic.[30]

## Black Magic

Black magic is the term used for magic that is performed for evil and/or self-serving purposes. Today, many people believe that Satan created black magic as a way to bring people closer to him and thereby trick them into becoming his followers. At one time, however, magic was considered a means of coming in contact with good angels. In the Middle Ages, a Jewish system of mystical philosophy and ritual called Cabala (also spelled Kabbalah) suggested that magic could be used to summon God's angels. Cabalists believed that God had given angels control of the natural world but ruled them by speaking their names. Consequently, Cabalists thought that if a magician spoke the names of angels in a certain way, using certain rituals, those angels could be controlled by the magician—not for evil, but for good. Although these names and rituals were not written down until the Middle Ages, medieval magicians were certain that they originated in the days of Adam and Eve, when an angel named Raziel gave Adam a book of spells and angel names as a gift. This book, the *Book of Raziel*, was eventually lost, but its teachings were passed down orally by Jews for generations.

The philosophical aspect of Cabala has recently gained more mainstream acceptability. The ritual aspect of Cabala is still practiced today, although it is generally considered an occult art rather than a part of the Jewish religion. The Bible forbids people from using sorcery, so Cabalists are often said to be worshiping demons, even though they insist they are connecting with good angels instead. Moreover, both Jews and Christians teach that sorcery invites devils into one's presence regardless of the practitioner's intent. Consequently, there have been many stories of magicians succumbing to Satan's temptations. For example, the sixteenth-century English playwright Christopher Marlowe and the nineteenth-century German poet Johann Wolfgang von Goethe both wrote plays based on legends about a sixteenth-century German magician, Dr. Johann Faust, who was said to have made a deal with the devil Mephistopheles, in which he exchanged his soul for twenty-four years of pleasure, wealth, and power.

## Dangerous Angels

Because an association with devils—real or imagined—can be harmful, some people are afraid to call on heavenly angels for help, fearing that a bad angel will appear instead of a good one. In their view, since Satan is a master of disguise, he and his followers would easily be able to trick someone into believing they are good angels. This fear that bad angels commonly masquerade as good ones was expressed in the first American book written on the subject of angels, the 1696 *Angelographia* by Increase Mather, which warned people about the dangers of associating with any angel. In discussing Mather's work, Eileen Freeman reports that Mather's concern still exists; in fact, she shares it herself. She says:

*Written in 1636, the story of Dr. Johann Faust depicts a magician who succumbs to the Devil's temptations.*

PLATE XIII.

# THE
# HISTORIE
### OF
# THE DAMNABLE
### LIFE, AND DESERVED
#### DEATH OF DOCTOR
##### *I OHN FAVSTVS.*

Newly printed, and in conuenient places, imperfect matter amended : according to the true Copie printed at *Frankfort*; and tranflated into Englifh, By *P. R.* Gent.

Printed at London ror *John Wright*, and are to be fold at the Signe of the *Bible* in *Gihfpar-Street* without Newgate. 1636.

FAUSTUS.
Historie of the Damnable Life and deserved Death of Faustus. London, 1636.
See Item No. 145.

Even today, many people counsel caution on the subject of angelic encounters, because of the deceptive powers of the dark. I have been to angel focus groups where the leader began by stating that only angels of light were welcome; after that the group made no attempt to examine whether the messages they received could possibly have been a deception. Merely wishing only for good angels to appear cannot guarantee it will be so.[31]

However, Freeman adds that while it can be hard to tell bad angels from good, it is not impossible, because there are discernible differences between encounters with each type of angel. She explains:

> Dark angels can only counterfeit the angels of the Light to a certain degree. They simply don't have it in them to enable a person to grow toward the Light, or to feel true love and joy, because they don't know what such things are any longer. They cannot produce anything but counterfeit fruits, and these break down and become bitter very quickly. Usually they don't even try to conquer our minds with evil per se. Instead they seduce us into worshipping ourselves and our gifts, as though we created ourselves and gave ourselves the abilities we have.[32]

Because good angels offer so many benefits to human beings, many people are willing to call on angels regardless of the risk of being tricked by a devil. Moreover, such people think that angels are a necessary comfort in a world where evil constantly threatens to disrupt lives. According to Richard Woods, a Dominican priest, "Angels are reassurance that the supernatural and the realm of God are real."[33] According to this view, distancing oneself from angels offers a greater risk than temptation from Satan; it means distancing oneself from God.

# A Matter of Faith

Ultimately, a belief in angels and all things related to angels can be based only on faith. No one can be certain about what these beings look like or how they act—if they exist at all. Therefore, some people might say it is foolish to believe in angels at all. Without proof of a thing's existence, such skeptics suggest, there is no point in trying to define its nature.

But believers in angels maintain that discussing angels brings them closer to God and to the common human experience of spirituality. To them, angels are the symbol of their faith, a reflection of the best qualities that humans share. As Karen Goldman, in her book *The Angel Book*, says:

> There is an unmistakable and profound reason why every culture, every religion, every nation down through the ages and in every part of the world extols angels as fit representations of man's highest conception of love and goodwill. They affect our highest senses, inspire our noblest thoughts, reflect our greatest aspirations. It is because at the core of our humanity we are really all very much alike on this earth, not in our animal-ness and mortality alone, but in our spirit.[34]

Moreover, believers in angels say that while there is no scientific proof that angels exist, stories of angel encounters provide ample evidence for their existence. When skeptics protest that they themselves have never seen an angel, some believers counter that only people who believe in angels are able to see them. For example, the Rev. John Westerhoff of Duke University suggests that a person who doubts the existence of any type of supernatural being will not recognize an angel even if one appears before him. He says:

> Angels exist through the eyes of faith, and faith is perception. Only if you can perceive it can you experience it. For some, their faith doesn't have room for such creatures. That's not to demean their faith. That's just the way they are; they can't believe things that aren't literal, that are outside the five senses.[35]

Most people, however, do have the sort of faith that allows them to accept the reality of angels without proof. For example, the Rev. Billy Graham explains his own belief in angels by saying:

> I do not believe in angels because someone has told me about a dramatic visitation from an angel, impressive as such rare testimonies may be. I do not believe in angels because UFOs are astonishingly angel-like in some of their reported appearances. I do not believe in angels because ESP [extrasensory perception] experts are making the realm of the spirit world seem more and more plausible. I do not believe in angels because of the sudden worldwide emphasis on the reality of Satan and demons. I do not believe in angels because I have ever seen one— because I haven't. I believe in angels because the

*Reverend Billy Graham believes, as many people do, that angels exist.*

Bible says there are angels; and I believe the Bible to be the true Word of God. I also believe in angels because I have sensed their presence in my life on special occasions.[36]

Graham's position represents the most common view in America today: Angels are present in people's lives, whether they are seen or unseen, and they exist regardless of whether or not people have accurately defined their activities.

# Notes

## Chapter 1: Where Did Angels Come From?

1. James R. Lewis and Evelyn Dorothy Oliver, *Angels A to Z*. ed. Kelle S. Sisung. Detroit: Visible Ink Press, 1996, p. 236.

## Chapter 2: What Do Angels Look Like?

2. Sophy Burnham, *A Book of Angels*. New York: Ballantine Books, 1990, pp. 117–18.
3. Quoted in Karen Armstrong, *Muhammad: A Biography of the Prophet*. San Francisco: HarperSanFrancisco, 1992, p. 83.
4. James Underhill, *Angels*. Shaftesbury, England: Element Books, 1995, p. 56.
5. Underhill, *Angels*, p. 20.
6. Quoted in Lewis and Oliver, *Angels A to Z*, p. 281.
7. Jay Stevenson, *The Complete Idiot's Guide to Angels*. New York: Alpha Books, 1999, pp. 308–9.
8. Quoted in Lewis and Oliver, *Angels A to Z*, p. 415.
9. Quoted in Lewis and Oliver, *Angels A to Z*, p. 415.
10. Malcolm Godwin, *Angels: An Endangered Species*. New York: Simon and Schuster, 1990, pp. 165–66.
11. Godwin, *Angels: An Endangered Species*, p. 166.
12. Godwin, *Angels: An Endangered Species*, p. 166.
13. Quoted in Joseph Fielding Smith, *Essentials in Church History*. Salt Lake City: Deseret Book Co., 1971, p. 44.
14. Lewis and Oliver, *Angels A to Z*, p. 102.
15. Eileen Elias Freeman, *Touched by Angels: True Cases of Close Encounters of the Celestial Kind*. New York: Warner Books, 1993, pp. 37–38.
16. Howard G. Chua-Eoan, "Sympathy for the Devil," *Time*, Dec. 27, 1993, p. 60.

## Chapter 3: What Do Good Angels Do?

17. Sophy Burnham, *A Book of Angels*. New York: Ballantine Books, 1990, pp. 234-35.
18. Janice T. Connell, *Angel Power*. New York: Ballantine Books, 1995, p. 182.
19. Godwin, *Angels: An Endangered Species*, p. 25.
20. Connell, *Angel Power*, p. 191.
21. Godwin, *Angels: An Endangered Species*, p. 32.
22. Connell, *Angel Power*, p. 100.
23. Nancy Gibbs, "Angels Among Us," *Time*, December 27, 1993, p. 59.
24. Gibbs, "Angels Among Us," p. 59.
25. Quoted in Gibbs, "Angels Among Us," p. 60.

## Chapter 4: Devils: What Do Bad Angels Do?

26. Godwin, *Angels: An Endangered Species*, p. 131.

27. Quoted in Lee Ann Chearney, ed., *The Quotable Angel*. New York: John Wiley and Sons, 1995, p. 105.

28. Godwin, *Angels: An Endangered Species*, p. 131.

29. Billy Graham, *Angels: Ringing Assurance That We Are Not Alone*. Dallas: Word Publishing, 1995, p. 104.

30. Stevenson, *The Complete Idiot's Guide to Angels*, p. 64.

31. Freeman, *Touched by Angels,* pp. 185–86.

32. Freeman, *Touched by Angels*, p. 186.

33. Quoted in Gibbs, "Angels Among Us," p. 59.

**Conclusion**: **A Matter of Faith**

34. Karen Goldman, *The Angel Book*. New York: Simon and Schuster, 1992, p. 16.

35. Quoted in Gibbs, "Angels Among Us," p. 60.

36. Graham, *Angels: Ringing Assurance That We Are Not Alone*, pp. 19–20.

# For Further Reading

Joan Wester Anderson, *An Angel to Watch over Me: True Stories of Children's Encounters with Angels*. New York: Ballantine Books, 1996. This book offers accounts of angel encounters reported by children.

Sophy Burnham, *Angel Letters*. New York: Ballantine Books, 1991. This book presents letters from people who believe they have encountered angels.

Helen Haidle, *Angels in Action*. Nashville: Thomas Nelson, 1996. This book, for readers age nine to twelve, provides information about angel encounters throughout history and discusses modern beliefs regarding angels.

Jordan Horowitz, *Angels in the Outfield*. New York: Disney Press, 1994. This novel is based on the 1994 Disney movie *Angels in the Outfield*.

Nathalie Ladner-Bischoff, *An Angel's Touch: True Stories About Angels, Miracles, and Answers to Prayer*. Nampa, Indiana: Pacific Press, 1998. This book offers reports of miracles that have occurred in response to prayers to God and/or guardian angels.

David R. Veerman, James C. Galin, and James C. Wilhoit, *104 Questions Children Ask About Heaven and Angels*. Ed. Daryl Lucas. Wheaton, Illinois: Tyndale House, 1996. This book for young people answers questions about angels from the Christian perspective.

# Works Consulted

Karen Armstrong, *Muhammad: A Biography of the Prophet*. San Francisco: Harper-SanFrancisco, 1992. Armstrong offers an in-depth biography of the Islamic prophet Muhammad.

Sophy Burnham, *A Book of Angels*. New York: Ballantine Books, 1990. This book presents historical and cultural information about angels and offers many stories of modern angel encounters.

Lee Ann Chearney, ed., *The Quotable Angel*. New York: John Wiley and Sons, 1995. Chearney presents numerous quotes from various types of literature that mention angels.

Janice T. Connell, *Angel Power*. New York: Ballantine Books, 1995. Connell discusses prevailing beliefs about the nature and duties of angels as well as her own beliefs about and experiences with angels.

Howard G. Chua-Eoan, "Sympathy for the Devil," *Time*, Dec. 27, 1993. Chua-Eoan discusses past and present opinions of Satan.

*The Essential Koran*. Trans. Thomas Cleary. San Francisco: HarperSanFrancisco, 1993. The Koran is the book of scriptures for the Islamic faith.

Eileen Elias Freeman, *Touched by Angels: True Cases of Close Encounters of the Celestial Kind*. New York: Warner Books, 1993. Freeman presents many stories of angel encounters in modern times.

Nancy Gibbs, "Angels Among Us," *Time*, December 27, 1993. Gibbs talks about angel beliefs in modern America.

Malcolm Godwin, *Angels: An Endangered Species*. New York: Simon and Schuster, 1990. For more advanced readers, this book provides historical and theological information about angels and discusses various theories related to their origin and nature.

Karen Goldman, *The Angel Book*. New York: Simon and Schuster, 1992. This slim volume summarizes modern beliefs in angels and talks about how people might get in touch with their own "inner angel."

Billy Graham, *Angels: Ringing Assurance That We Are Not Alone*. Dallas: Word Publishing, 1995. Protestant minister Graham discusses his own belief in angels and provides descriptions and angel stories from other believers throughout history.

The Holy Bible: Authorized (King James) Version. New York: American Bible Society. The Bible is a book of scriptures for the Jewish and Christian faiths. The King James version is the most widely used translation for English-speaking Protestants.

James R. Lewis and Evelyn Dorothy Oliver, *Angels A to Z*. Ed. Kelle S. Sisung. Detroit: Visible Ink Press, 1996. This encyclopedia provides information on how good and bad angels have been presented in mythology, folklore, art, literature, and religion throughout history.

Joseph Fielding Smith, *Essentials in Church History*. Salt Lake City: Deseret Book Co., 1971. This book presents information about the Mormon Church, as provided by its founder.

Jay Stevenson, *The Complete Idiot's Guide to Angels*. New York: Alpha Books, 1999. Stevenson offers in-depth information about the history of angels, as well as theological and popular views of both good and bad angels.

James Underhill, *Angels*. Shaftesbury, England: Element Books, 1995. This book provides historical information about angels, along with many color photographs depicting angel artwork throughout history.

# Index

# Picture Credits

# About the Author

Patricia D. Netzley is the author of over two dozen books for children and adults. Her works include *The Curse of King Tut* (Lucent Books), *The Encyclopedia of Movie Special Effects* (Oryx Press), and *Environmental Literature: An Encyclopedia of Works, Authors, and Themes* (ABC-Clio). Netzley has been a freelance author since 1986, after spending six years as an editor for the UCLA Medical Center in Los Angeles, California. She currently lives in Southern California with her husband Raymond and their three children, Matthew, Sarah, and Jacob.